voiceJunction
SATB and piano

OXFORD

Marie-Claire Saindon

# Fingernail Moon

Difficulty level ● ● ◑ ○

# Fingernail Moon

Paul Grindlay (b. 1965)

MARIE-CLAIRE SAINDON

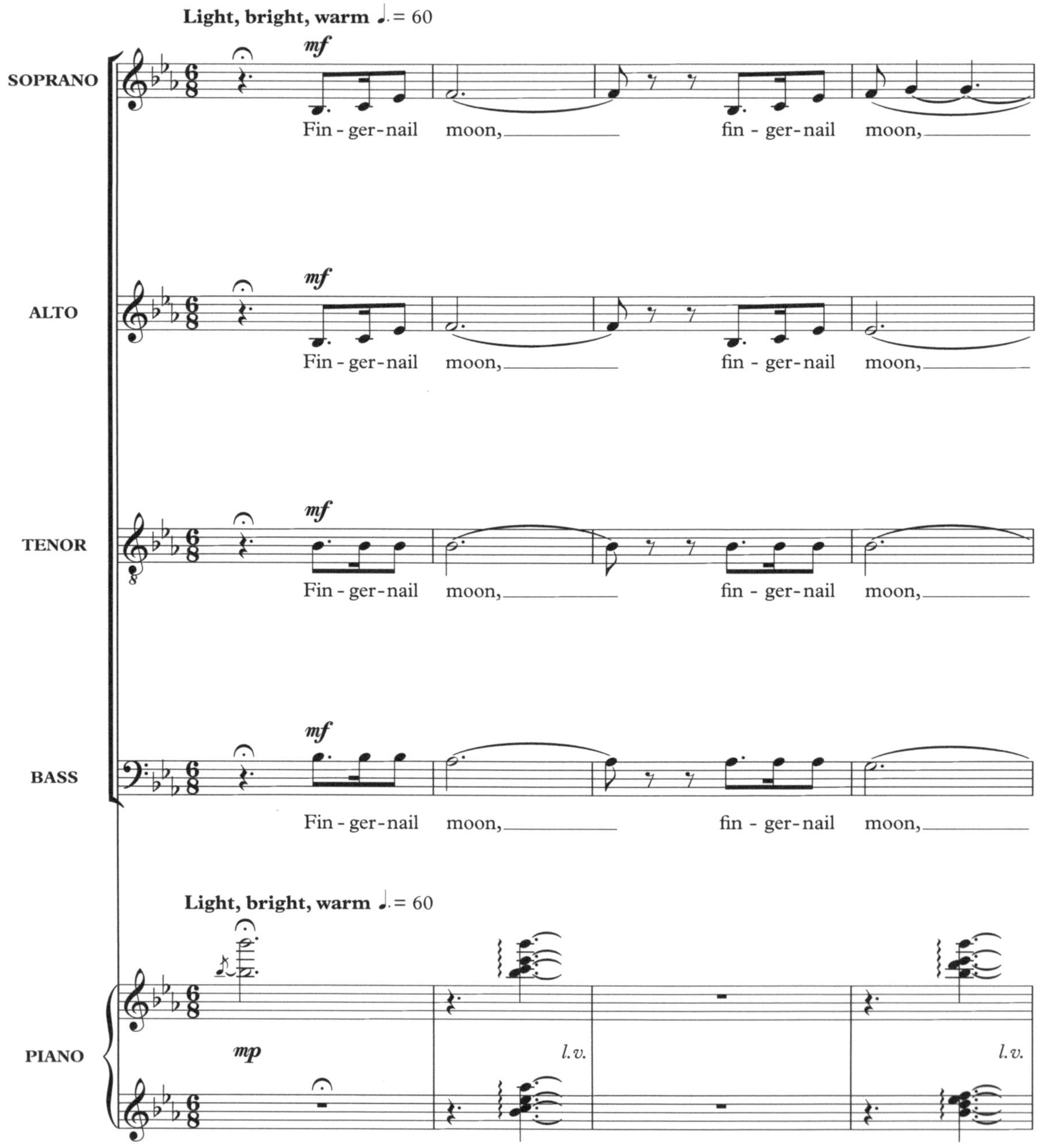

**Light, bright, warm** ♩. = 60

SOPRANO

*mf*

Fin - ger-nail moon,_____ fin - ger - nail moon,_____

ALTO

*mf*

Fin - ger-nail moon,_____ fin - ger - nail moon,_____

TENOR

*mf*

Fin - ger-nail moon,_____ fin - ger - nail moon,_____

BASS

*mf*

Fin - ger-nail moon,_____ fin - ger - nail moon,_____

**Light, bright, warm** ♩. = 60

PIANO

*mp*

*l. v.*

*l. v.*

SSA version commissioned by Oriana Women's Choir (Mitchell Pady, Artistic Director)

OXFORD UNIVERSITY PRESS, MUSIC DEPARTMENT, GREAT CLARENDON STREET, OXFORD OX2 6DP
The Moral Rights of the Composer have been asserted. Photocopying this copyright material is ILLEGAL.

6

down here be - low, what should I learn

learn down here be- low, down here be - low, what should I

What should I learn down here be - low,

down here be - low, what should I learn

or know a - bout the

learn or know a - bout the

what should I learn or know a - bout the

or know a - bout the

un - earth - ly glow, the un - earth - ly glow_____ of your

un - earth - ly glow, the un - earth - ly glow_____ of your

un - earth - ly glow, the un - earth - ly glow_____ of your

un - earth - ly glow, the un - earth - ly glow_____ of your

lu - - - - - nar light show?_____

lu - - - - - nar light show?_____

lu - - - - - nar light show?_____

lu - - - - - nar light show?_____

14

# voiceJunction

Voice Junction is an inspirational concert series for all modern mixed-voice singing groups. A meeting point of various styles, the series is fresh, popular, and alternative in feel, and includes new original works—both accompanied and *a cappella*—alongside unique arrangements of well-known tunes. Whether performed by a one-per-part vocal group or a community choir, this is music that brings people together.

Marie-Claire Saindon is a Franco-Ontarian composer with a penchant for vivid imagery and a great affinity for setting text. In addition to her role as composer-in-residence for Chœur Adleisia, she runs creative choral and vocal composition workshops, scores films, and teaches Irish fiddle. Her choral works have been performed in many countries, continents, and contexts, from local community performances to the World Symposium on Choral Music, and have been awarded multiple prizes for composition.

Photo: Richmond Lam

www.oup.com

ISBN 978-0-19-357924-8